"A short, but powerfully moving account of the author's tumultuous journey towards forgiveness and grace amid life's indelible challenges. Centered on the resiliency of serving in a volatile combat zone, she shares her personal awaking that we all must realize for ourselves; the need to take down the purpose-built armor and allow yourself to be vulnerable—truly vulnerable. She takes us along on an enlightening excursion of relationships, trust, love, death, and forgiveness that forces one to reflect on one's own battles and demons to ultimately enter and center on the profoundness and simplicity of grace. Take a moment to renew your spirit in this wonderful read which beautifully re-calibrates one's mind in the things you know, need to learn, or simply remind yourself of. Simply stated, this book is re-charge for the soul."

—*Ellen Tannor Richardson*

*Life is meant to be lived courageously,
it is a marathon not a sprint.*

The Coefficient of *Grace*

Rena Patierno

The Coefficient of Grace

Copyright © 2020, Rena Patierno. All rights reserved.

Cover Design: Fantasy & Coffee Design

Editor: Tiffany White

Book Design: Laura Scott, Book Love Space

ISBN 978-1-7357634-0-8

v. 1.0.1

This is my command—be strong and courageous! Do not be afraid or discouraged. For the LORD your God is with you wherever you go.

Joshua 1:9, NLT

For my mom and dad. Hummingbirds are beautiful birds that can to fly in all directions, drink in the nectar of life, and hover just long enough to be simply present in the moment.

Preface

> "Maybe this one moment, with this one person, is the very reason we're here on Earth at this time."
>
> —*Jean Watson*

Life is filled with joyfulness, love, peace, and harmony. Anyone can achieve a life of harmony and balance, but you must embrace the journey with clarity and purpose: it is a marathon, not a sprint. Life is about being courageous and brave. Living requires commitment to learning about yourself and a perseverance and dedication to control your anxiety and fear. Anxiety causes self-doubt and prevents you from moving forward with a joyful heart. Once you begin to acknowledge fear, manage anxiety, and learn to calm your inner self, you then can discover grace and forgiveness. Grace and forgiveness of self will help you to embrace life as a series of controllable events. Your life is the constant, and how you live it is about managing the variables.

I hope this book touches your heart and provides awareness for your journey—whatever that journey is. God bless and God speed!

Introduction

The Coefficient of Grace is a product of many years of living, existing, and just passing through. These were years of hurting, healing, and resiliency. As I reflected on life, I felt a gravitational pull to expand knowledge of myself, of choices, and of the relationships between human beings. During this period of exploration and healing, I learned to appreciate the spaces in between life events.

As I began to search my soul for a title for this book, I harkened back to my days of watercolor painting and the freedom of expression it provided. I was reminded of abstract art and how it represents reality by using colors and forms without attempting to represent an accurate version of the truth. This is much like life and the lens with which we choose to see the world. Understanding life as a series of events and how we manage these events reminded me of algebra and coefficients.

In algebra, the coefficient is the number by which you multiply. For example, 5 is the coefficient in the equation $5x = y$. For the purpose of this book, life is multiplied by its variables. Variables are experiences and feelings. These variables occur in seconds, minutes, hours. They are cumulative, and how we manage them equates to the balance and quality of living.

Life Multiplied by Variables = Your Journey

The core of a joyful life is managing variables. Take responsibility for you, change the lens, and broaden the optic to visualize life differently.

I began developing the concept of a book upon my return from Afghanistan in November of 2010. The initial concept was generated out of my frustration with the lack of a realistic transition program

Introduction

to assist reserve service members in shifting back to civilian life.

United States Army Reserve soldiers perform two days per month and two weeks per year, sprinkled with a 365-day deployment here and there. In my eighteen years, I have mobilized five times, deployed to Afghanistan, and completed an additional three-year tour on active duty, for grand total of approximately ten years—or half of my reserve career, not the typical trajectory for an Army reserve solider. It's an easy transition when performing only two days per month. However, deployment in a combat zone is a different story, and transitioning back to civilian life is not so seamless.

My transition to and from the combat zone in November 2010 went something like this: civilian to active duty at a mobilization station for ninety-plus days; boots on the ground in Afghanistan for a nine-month combat tour; return home. At the end of the tour, I recall arriving at the air terminal in Indianapolis in the cover of darkness. About seventy-five members of the 404th Civil Affairs Battalion disembarked the plane after a sixteen-hour flight.

THE COEFFICIENT OF GRACE

The air was cold, damp, and the smell of jet fuel filled the air. We were directed to grab our bags from the belly of the aircraft and move in an orderly fashion into the cargo terminal holding area. Once inside, the first sergeant called the room to attention and barked, "I know many of you have family members waiting for you on post, but you are ordered to not engage, socialize, or visit with them, period. If you do, you will answer to the commander, and trust me, that will not bode well for you. Now gather your things and wait for the bus to transport us back to Camp Atterbury. Additional instructions will be provided once on post."

The room was still and the silence deafening. The announcement was disheartening. Welcome home and thank you for your service! Any pride for what we had done, any hope to see our loved ones, was gone. Keep in mind it is 0300, there was no USO, no coffee, no food, nothing. I was taken aback. I remember looking to my left and my right and thinking how mentally, physically, and emotionally tired the soldiers appeared—including myself. My hair was gray, my face tired and weary, and my eyes without a sparkle.

Introduction

I hardly recognized me. I just wanted to be home to see my family and my two dogs.

It took ninety days of intensive training to prepare mentally, emotionally, and physically to deploy, and only four days to demobilize. The unit was required to attend countless mandatory post-deployment briefings. In between briefings, meals, and sleep, we had mandatory formations to avoid any chance of free time. It became clear the goal was to have everyone who returned home from Afghanistan back to their home of record no later than Wednesday, the day before Thanksgiving, regardless of medical, emotional, or spiritual challenges. I was shocked and aghast at this schedule. Keep in mind, none of us had seen or engaged with our families, but too exhausted to challenge the process, we kept quiet and followed orders. Whenever possible, we attempted to explain to family members via cellphone that we would see them after training had been completed, not before, or we'd run the risk of reprimand for not following orders. Most families were angry but had little to no recourse as senior leaders were not accessible. A change of command had occurred during our time in Afghanistan, and the new leaders were unfamiliar and clearly not to be trusted. After an intense four days, everyone was officially released from active duty to return home after a year away.

I was home from the demobilization station for roughly two weeks before returning to my civilian job. I was comfortable going back to what was typical, which was nursing. It was a safe and familiar place. However, home didn't feel like home. It was conflicted and full of contention and drama. I longed to be back in a combat zone, where life was filled with simpler variables: I had actionable tasks, mission planning, and deliverable products, a place where feelings were not allowed.

I continued to work as a nurse over the next year, where comfort became the standard. I was working four shifts per week, which were twelve-hour days, performing Army training one weekend a month, and seeing my husband at the convenience of his schedule. This was the new normal. What was not normal was my inability to sleep more than four hours a night, yet being comforted by the sound of helicopters and random gunfire. Anyone who has served in a combat zone understands.

Introduction

It took two years for me to realize I was repressing my feelings and struggling with emotional transitions; my anger and frustration persisted regarding the events at the demobilization site. Completely out of sorts, filled with anxiety and fear, I searched for a place to fit in. I continued to have trouble sleeping, my marriage was failing, and I felt stuck in a sea of hopelessness. I was the rock of the family, the strong, sensible critical thinker whom everyone needed, so out of guilt for being gone, I carried the additional weight in my rucksack and pushed forward, but never saw the shore or safe harbor for myself. Life moved fast and I was running to keep up. Feelings of imperfection and failure, and the many combat experiences, survived in my heart and languished in my soul. Finding a way to stay strong during this downward spiral of constant change was a challenge, and I sought to understand this unfamiliar space by grasping for solutions.

One day I awoke earlier than normal and decided to run to clear my head. About two miles into the run, I started thinking about the magnificent brain. The old brain and the new brain. The old brain is the unconscious portion, where fear and threat detection are housed. The new brain has many parts. However, the prefrontal cortex is where personality development, critical thinking, planning, strategizing, and moral reasoning occurs. The prefrontal cortex is especially important in controlling reflexive behavior responses and self-control. The old brain is in charge, and the new brain is its slave, *i.e.*, the fight-or-flight response. Imagine the elephant, big and strong, and the mouse, very tiny in comparison. We cannot live our lives riding on the elephant, always in fear. It is important to live with purpose and clarity, not in fear.

I was living in a continuous state of fight-or-flight, a never-ending loop of negative emotional hell, unable to utilize the prefrontal cortex. I am a soldier—trained, ready, and resilient—and quitting was not an option. Could this be all there was to life? I prayed not.

Breaking free from this emotional hell was arduous. I was in a small boat, looking up, constantly paddling upstream; there was no ebb and flow in my life, just constant change and emotional discord. I believed that filling my wells by nurturing and caring for people could break the negative emotional cycle. However, there was lack of a recurrent rhythmical pattern or

Introduction

regrowth, just an ongoing decline. Filling my life with stuff was an emotional response to emptiness and ongoing strife. Everything I did was driven by my ancient brain, my emotional responses founded in fight-or-flight. Nothing I did originated in critical thought or reasoning. This was counter to what I knew life to be prior to deployment. I found myself placing an emphasis on things that defined me or completed me, which provided a sense of safety. I strived for normal, rational, unemotional thought. Life needed to be about finding my way back to my former self. What did this mean? Simply, to have the ebb and flow of life return; to be my best self in my many roles as a daughter, sister, niece, aunt, wife, and nurse. I paused, and realized I was lost in change; I didn't know Rena any longer. This is where the journey to a joyful heart and a harmonious life begins.

Afghanistan

From November of 2009 until November of 2010, I was placed on active duty and deployed to Afghanistan as the Civil Affairs Team (CAT A) leader assigned to the Kapisa Provincial Reconstruction Team (PRT). The PRT mission was to stabilize the region by enabling local governments to care for, educate, employ, and protect its people through the construction of basic infrastructure and mentorship programs while conducting counterinsurgency and stability operations. Kapisa was and continues to be the gateway to Kabul and is known for high insurgent activity. During 2010, Kapisa was under operational control of Region Command East and 101st Airborne Division. In addition, the Kapisa Area of Operations was under the control of Task Force Lafayette, commanded by a French two-star general.

I was a female Army nurse corps officer in Afghanistan, working with the 101st Airborne Division, French forces, the Department of State, USAID, international organizations, and national governmental organizations, among other entities. The experience was surreal and pivotal in my life, but it would take me years to know and understand the impact.

From early March until the end of May 2010, I was the lead writer of the women's portion of the Kapisa campaign plan and was assigned as team lead for American and French female engagement teams. One day in late May 2010, I was called by the Air Force PRT commander and told I was being sent forward to Forward Operating Base (FOB) Tora, in the Surobi District. General Chavancy, commander of French forces, requested I be moved forward to support French civil military teams on the FOB Tora. The area of Surobi is located approximately sixty kilometers east of Kabul and has a high number of

Taliban fighters. Taliban activity and land mines left over from the Russian occupation made travel difficult and life-threatening; roadside bombs and ambush attacks were commonplace. I was honored, yet apprehensive, by this unexpected and unplanned move. I did not have time for discussions or mission planning and was given fifteen minutes to gather my belongings and get on a French helicopter for the journey south. My apprehension was founded out of concern as the French military elements were under direct command and control of the 2nd Parachute Regiment of the French Foreign Legion, and I would be the only U.S. Officer on the FOB and on the staff.

The helicopters landed and the rotors continued to spin. The French Air crew grabbed bags, threw them into the aircraft, and we took off. The helicopters flew with doors open, guns manned, and I remember thinking what a beautiful country. However, I was quickly reminded of the hell and fury on the ground below. The landscape had been ravaged and demolished by thirty years of war, which had clearly taken its toll on the land and the people. We flew for about twenty-five minutes, making sure to avoid the Tagab region—another Taliban hot spot where frequent rocket-propelled grenades were launched against any coalition aircraft.

The helicopter landed at FOB Tora and I was met by the Civil-Military Cooperation counterpart. A French Army officer, Captain Franz Najean, who spoke English, welcomed me to the "highway to hell" while drinking a coffee and smoking a cigarette. I was ordered to report to the regiment commander's office and told not to worry because the regiment commander spoke English and was a nice guy—as far as legionnaires went. On the long walk from the landing zone in one hundred-degree heat, carrying all of my gear to include my assigned weapons, we discussed daily schedule and quarters. Once inside the tactical operations center, I met the operations officer, a formidable Frenchman, but I sensed a kind heart. He shook my hand and welcomed me with a smirk. The regiment commander, Colonel des Minières, stood in the doorway to his office to welcome me and assured me he spoke English. He commanded all company commanders to treat me as a member of the senior staff, and he followed by saying "Let me put your fears to rest, I speak English and have instructed all of the company commanders to accept you and treat you as a member of the Senior Staff." I breathed a huge sigh of relief. We immediately began to talk business and the way forward for coordination of efforts between French and U.S. projects in the area.

Later that evening, I was introduced to Task Force Altor's company commanders, none of whom spoke English. Intimidating to say the least. Franz Najean and Sebastien Kravitz, my new battle buddies, spoke great English and acted as my interpreters. During my first week on the FOB, I was introduced to a communications officer who offered daily French lessons. I had two hours of French per day, and within in a week I was part of the task force, briefing the command in French on U.S. projects in the area that assisted with identification of new projects to support current counterinsurgency operations.

The French Foreign Legion has a lengthy history steeped in traditions. I learned much about leadership, discipline, integrity, and the human consequence. Officers are expected to participate in all the traditions of Legion, including ceremonies and dining traditions. That means lieutenants sit with lieutenants, captains sit with captains, and field grade officers sit with the commander. I did what was expected and ate all lunches and dinners with the captains. I was respected as command staff and reported directly to Regiment Commander. It was a huge honor to stand side by side with French soldiers, many of whom had served in Bosnia, Djibouti, and the Central African Republic.

In early July 2010, Task Force Altor transitioned out of Afghanistan and was followed by Task Force (TF) Bison. TF Bison was commanded by a French officer, who like the previous commander welcomed me to his staff. Another combat chapter had begun. I continued to support French and American counterinsurgency and stability operation efforts in the Surobi for the remainder of my tour. I also worked closely with the U.S. special operations teams and provided female support to their missions.

One evening around 2300, I was summoned urgently to the operation's center by the Task Force commander. There had been rocket fire on Common Outpost (COP) Rocco, and one of the French nurses had been seriously injured. The French medical team were in the operations center and asked me for my professional assessment of the situation. French nurses are more like our special operations medics than actual registered nurses, such as in the United States. I feared the worst for the nurse. Knowing what a close-range rocket impact can do to the human body, I offered my critical care and trauma nursing skills to the medical team. The center was silent as everyone waited for a report from the outpost forty kilometers away. A call was placed to French Air assets located at the Kabul International Airport. The flight from Kabul to the COP would take approximately fifteen minutes. The request was for medevac and close air support helicopters, specifically two French attack helicopters known as Tigers and a NH90 Super Puma. The silence in the operations center was shattered by the launching of mechanized artillery rounds in response to the insurgents' rocket attack. The ground shook and the shock waves could be felt for seconds after the rounds left the tube. It seemed like hours before the medevac and escort helicopters flew over our base to the site of tragedy. The operations center remained deathly quiet. Finally, a radio transmission broke the silence, and the French pilot's voice was tenuous and hesitant. Patient was in route to the FOB, but the medical team would need to meet the medevac helicopter on the landing zone. I knew what this meant, as did the medical team. We ran to the clinic, grabbed medical supplies and resuscitative equipment, and headed to the landing zone. The medevac landed in minutes. It was a horrific sight, but not unfamiliar to myself or the medical team. The nurse was in grave condition, and despite our efforts, he later passed. Out of my nine months in Afghanistan, I attended ten French funerals, all humbling and emotionally challenging. The year 2010 was the largest loss of life for the French military since the bombing in Lebanon in 1983. The loss of life was difficult to reconcile, and it would take years to find peace in the stillness of my heart.

Despite the bad times, I have many great memories of Afghanistan. The Afghans are a wonderful people, simple and kind. During my assignment, I supported key elements in numerous interagency personnel, most notably USAID, Department of State, Department of Agriculture, United States Army Corps of Engineers, all in the name of security operations. I worked directly with provincial leaders and senior representatives of the Afghanistan government to assist in developing programs supported by coalition forces and interagency personnel. I also worked directly with Ministry of Public Health initiatives for clean water projects and strong foods programs for malnourished women and children. Another of my noteworthy projects was the School of Nursing in the Parwan Province. The mortality rates during childbirth in 2010 were extremely high and were correlated with the lack of access to doctors, the high rates of poverty, and other social- and cultural-related restrictions. These restrictions were part of the reason for creating the school.

People often ask if Afghanistan changed me. The answer is yes. But the answer is not a simple yes— it is a complex yes, and required living, loving, and losing to understand how it changed me. I needed to understand external change, the process of internal recalibration, and ultimately how to manage fear and anxiety.

Transitions

TRANSITIONS WERE THE REASONS I BEGAN WRITING, and it became apparent transitions were secondary to grace and forgiveness but necessary for a harmonious life and a joyful heart. The transitions I experienced were emotional. Emotional transitions are lifelong processes that are important to successful life changes. Transitions are internal, whereas change is external. Transitions are internal reconfigurations in response to external changes and are done consciously and unconsciously, and at some point, mine became contentious.

Somewhere during 2012, it became obvious that changes and emotional transitions were something all of us do every day; it was not present simply in my change from military to civilian, but in every role in my life. For example, military to civilian, civilian job to wife, mom, etc.

In 2013, an old friend who had known me in the early 2000s and whom I was seeing again for the first time since returning home from Afghanistan said something I won't ever forget: "Rena you've lost your smile, and the bright light in our heart that everyone loved has gone dark." He also told me I was hard, distant, and unreachable. Those words were incredibly hard to hear, but in my heart, I knew he was speaking the truth. I had armored up and blocked all things, including my own vulnerability. My emotional transitions provoked negativity, frustration, and anger. Going from being Rena the person, the nurse, the wife, or the Army officer and back to Rena was a process. I could either do it gracefully or begrudgingly.

After many hours on the beach, pondering the uncomplicated balance and grace of the sea, I looked deep within myself and expanded my awareness, sharpened my attention to detail, and made a choice to transform my future. I had lost me once before, when

Transitions

I was in my early thirties, and I promised myself I would never allow that to happen again.

Through the help of my dear friend and therapist Pat Powers, I began the journey to manage change, grieve loss, stand in the chaos, and embrace new beginnings. This was a process of self-discovery and self-actualization. This life's journey has led me to understand grace and forgiveness, first for myself, and then for others.

This journey was painful, with many frequent changes and the need to manage complex emotional events. Adapting to new circumstances can be mentally and emotionally exhausting. During the quiet pauses of adaptation and self-reflection, I had to learn why and how certain variables triggered my emotional responses, and why it was necessary for me to set boundaries. Letting go of grief, dismantling old perspectives, and bridging change was the new way forward. I had clarity and experienced newfound feelings of grace, forgiveness, and a joyful heart.

As adults we have the ability to control our emotional transitions. However, identifying external change events and knowing when we armor up is essential. Try to stand still in the chaos and understand the emotional confusion and anxiety. Pause and allow opportunities for the de-escalation of feelings and clarity. Time and patience are crucial to allow new ideas and short-term goals to arise. This all begins with self-reflection and appreciation of change. Study change and embrace grace.

Grace

GRACE IMPLIES ELEGANCE, a beautiful and pleasing way of movement. It is also a polite and thoughtful way of behaving. What comes to mind when I hear the word grace? God, swans, ballerinas, gymnasts, swimmers, the tall grass blowing in the wind, or hummingbirds drinking in the precious nectar of life. Above all, grace is the sea. It's a tangible illustration of an uncomplicated balance. The ebb and flow of the sea, always giving and always receiving, comes from a place of extreme grace. From all these things, I have learned to be graceful and vulnerable, to love without expectation, and to care for others. I have cared for thousands of patients over the last twenty-six years, but there are a few who touched my heart with intensity and overwhelming kindness. They changed my heart and taught me grace and forgiveness.

In 2003, I cared for a patient named George. George was retired Navy, a quiet, unassuming hero. He was admitted to the intensive care unit after a lung resection with a diagnosis of pulmonary fibrosis. He was not able to breathe without ventilator support and was given a tracheostomy after fourteen days. George was implicit regarding his advance directives: he did not want artificial hydration or a permanent feeding tube and no life-sustaining heroic medical treatments. I cared for him and his family for four months. I remember leaving his room in the intensive care unit one day, and he began tapping fervently on the side-rail to get my attention. He wrote, "Please be here when I go home." He was writing on his bedside clipboard with great urgency and intent. "Please, promise me you will be here when I go home, and wear your uniform." I knew what this meant. George was preparing his final goodbyes. I took a deep breath and quieted his hand. This was a Tuesday, and the plan on Wednesday was to take him off the ventilator and place him on comfort measures. I remember explaining to family I had a final exam and most probably would not be present on Wednesday. I came to work on Thursday and was shocked to see George's name on the assignment board. I walked into the adjacent intensive care unit and into his room. With his wife and children at the bedside, George looked at me, reached for my hand, smiled, and passed away. His family told me he wouldn't leave without seeing me one last time. Standing at George's bedside was powerful. It was important in that moment to embrace the cycle of life and appreciate grace in its true unselfish form. It was one of my first experiences with grace, and definitely not my last. My life has been filled graceful moments since.

As an advance nurse practitioner specializing in hospital-based care and palliative/end-of-life care, understanding the human consequence is vital and central to gracefulness. My gift of caring for others is a blessing that requires critical thinking and setting emotional boundaries. Each person has their own fears, vulnerabilities, guilt, and protective mechanisms.

The Coefficient of Grace

Sitting in silence, in total vulnerability, and listening to another human being's story is hard but essential. I prayed many years ago to God to bless me with the skills of empathy, gracefulness, and compassion to do the job of nursing. I am happy to say after twenty-six years, I am still doing God's work with empathy, grace, compassion, and a greater understanding of the human consequence. I can still cry with patients and their families, and this is the graceful connection that allows me to remain humble.

I used to try and understand others' opinions regarding grace, but then I realized this was time and oxygen I would never get back. This is an individual journey, not a think tank. What I know is grace begins with self-reflection and understanding the fine balance between the ebb and flow of life. Grace comes from knowing what makes your heart sing, what brings you joy, and what makes you fearful. Once you can identify and eliminate feelings of fear and anxiety, you can calm your inner self, locate balance, and be graceful.

Make a promise to yourself to mitigate responding to anxiety and fear. Stand in graceful stillness. Breathe and find quietness within your mind, and balance yourself. Reflect on your feelings, employ rational thought, and choose when and how you respond. Not everything requires an immediate response, and some things don't require any response. Live life from a place of balance and vulnerability.

Vulnerability

VULNERABILITY CAN BE EXPLAINED as defenselessness or a state of unprotectiveness. Vulnerability is the ability to see yourself truthfully, embrace your shortcomings, and let go of the fears in your heart. Vulnerability is another essential element of a harmonious life. When you stop caring about what people think of you, you have lost your ability to be vulnerable. It is important what people think. However, what people think does not define who you are. It should not distract you from your purpose. It's easy to say "I don't care if you accept me," but that's probably not true. We really do care, and that allows us to remain vulnerable.

I met a very special man about a year ago who provided me safe harbor and taught me to be courageous and vulnerable with my heart. The following piece of writing was my first attempt at being vulnerable in many years: "I will carry the mental image of the contour of your face always. It will remain in a safe place, tucked away in a quiet remote place in my heart. This I promise! I will never let you fade away." I asked that very special man in my life if I could share my thoughts about him with him, and he said of course. I took a huge breath, checked my pulse, and then took another big breath and read the words. I was exposed and totally unprotected.

Being vulnerable requires being seen without any guarantee of results. Pause in your emotional state of fear and anxiety. If you find yourself filled with self-doubt, consumed with self-judging and self-deprecating thoughts that only perpetuate the cycle of anxiety and fear, pause and appreciate that this is the old brain, the fight-or-flight response. Fight-or-flight causes you to armor up, and armor provides protection

Vulnerability

but prevents vulnerability. Have courage through this fear and resist the urge to put on your armor. Take a deep breath, acknowledge the unconscious emotional response to fear, and begin to employ critical thinking. Acknowledge the fear and anxiety and implement positive self-talk.

Practice being vulnerable in any moment. This will leave you feeling unprotected and defenseless. Work on identifying fear, and seek to recognize emotional responses. It is in this exposed state that you begin to understand how to manage anxiety and apply critical thinking. Engage in purposeful thought while navigating the uncomfortable feelings. Take a step back and be candid with yourself. Feel the balance; it is about being graceful and kind in the most difficult times. Stand quiet in chaos and open your mind to clear and purposeful thought. Relearn your worth. Over the past three years I have come to understand that my contributions are bigger than myself. Selfless vulnerable service to my community, patients, and county.

Self-Trust

I HAVE SPENT NUMEROUS HOURS searching the spaces in between the events in my life, breathing, and seeking to understand trust. Trust is the basis around which all human relationships revolve. Trust is about continual life learning and exploring hope. Self-trust is the steady reliance on your own integrity. Self-trust is not knowing all of the answers or doing all things correctly. It is about the principle that you will be kind and respectful to yourself regardless of the outcome. Self-trust leads to the gift of peace in your heart and mind without punishment or regret. Buying into negative thoughts diminishes self-trust and facilitates living in the past. If we live in the past, in a state of conscious regret, we become fearful of the future. Bouncing back and forth between the past and the future means we miss the present. Missing the present means repeating past emotional cycles. In addition, missing the present also incites worry, which in turn increases anxiety and fear of vulnerability. The way to cultivate a courageous, trusting heart is to be fully in the present, eliminating fear and allowing for sanctuary. This harmony fosters self-trust, facilitates trusting others, and promotes loving freely without expectations.

The special man expressed to me on numerous occasions that "Life is about living in the moment and being present, 100 percent with the one you are with. It is not about distractions; it is about focus." This is extremely hard to do. The world is wired for distractions, and constant connectivity sets us up for failure. Trusting your connection with the person you are with, and trusting that person in your absence, is difficult if you continue to live in the past. Remain focused on your purpose. Do not allow the opinions of others to distract you. Stay

Self-Trust

focused, remain present, and manage the fear and anxiety.

In my personal life, I can openly admit, trust is a huge issue for me. I have had several experiences with people who were not honest and whose integrity was less than honorable. Trust was violated in my marriage and has become a stumbling block in my life. I love without expectation. I have had to learn to self-trust. Trust is a delicate gift, and when it is violated, the pain can isolate us from meaningful relationships. Over the past five years, it has been difficult to trust anyone with my heart or even allow them in my life. Moving forward from this pain required staying very aware of my past experiences and acknowledging when I began to feel anxious. I had to be true to myself while remaining strong and confident. Self-trust allows people in my scared space to see me. It's incredibly difficult to trust, but it is necessary for living. Learning self-trust is the time for being graceful, patient, and present with yourself. The goal of self-trust is to be vulnerable in all things. Be confident in who you are. I have learned to trust myself, as well as others.

The Coefficient of Grace

Seek to understand your strengths, weaknesses, and vulnerabilities. It is important to understand the person you are sharing space with is just as exposed as you—unprotected and vulnerable. You must pause and listen to your inside voice. Make the conscious decision to live focused and in the present. Choose to stand unarmored and completely vulnerable in the presence of gifts (people) in order to experience the true treasure each person brings to your life. Learn to understand how you respond to change and develop a courageous heart. It's also important to recognize symptoms of anxiety. I have learned to recognize when I am off balance and no longer harmonious with myself: my sleep patterns shift, I feel exhausted, I crave simple sugars, and I become filled with self-doubt and negative thoughts.

The lack of self-trust can be overwhelming. If you find yourself in that situation, find a quiet place, meditate, and focus on breathing in for a count of five and out for a count of five. Each inhalation and exhalation, feel the balance and harmony. Be in the present, experience the stillness and inner peace, and quiet the noise in the mind and heart. Learning to manage your inner

Self-Trust

voice frees up your energy to develop better self-trust. Remaining present will allow you to have balance and move forward with focused presence and clarity.

In addition, create your mantra. Mantras are affirmations that motivate and inspire you to be your best self. Write them on paper, the bathroom mirror, a place where you will be reminded daily, and read the words out loud. For example, *I am special, I am worthy, I am a good and honest person*, and *I am loved*—whatever your words may be.

Remember to be kind and patient with yourself. Have courage to give the love in your heart freely, knowing you might not be loved back. Trust is about sharing space and being your best self in that space. God has a plan for your life. For now, keep living gracefully and courageously.

Imperfections

THE IDEA OF BEING OF A PERFECT SOLIDER is not accepted or expected in the Army, but to admit imperfection requires vulnerability and courage. Post-traumatic stress disorder is an imperfection that necessitates courage to admit. PTSD carries a stigma. Most military members are hesitant to admit symptoms of PTSD and seek treatment because of fears of ruining their military careers. Leaders and mental health care providers say there is nothing shameful about mental health disorders, but this does not change the accompanying fears. Mental health issues, including PTSD, are challenging for both the military services and the person suffering.

The Coefficient of Grace

In August of 2019, I was in my home in upstate NY, asleep in my bed, and there was a horrific thunderstorm; I typically love thunderstorms, the sound of rolling thunder traveling throughout the Catskill Mountains, the rhythmic pinging of raindrops on the metal roof, flashes of lightning in the darkness. However, this storm was different. Loud cracks and pops exploded in the darkness. The lights flickered and the house shook, and eventually, the power went out. I have been in circumstances before where the power had gone out, but something was different. I was paralyzed with fear. My mind raced and my heart beat rapidly—fight-or-flight. I panicked because I could not figure out how to get my garage open without power. How would I get my car out and travel to work? How was I going to shower, make coffee? The thoughts raced in my mind, gaining speed with each iteration. My thoughts were completely out of control. I tried deep breathing, but nothing worked. This was panic. Desperate to calm my fears and alleviate my anxiety, I recalled my pre-deployment Humvee rollover training (HEAT).

The goal of HEAT is to increase the situational awareness of vehicle rollover by permitting the instructor to observe the performance of the team and their reactions to emergency conditions without requiring the use of an actual vehicle. The device reinforces the importance of seat positioning, wearing seatbelts, demonstrating the feeling of being disoriented, and the actual effort required to execute rollover procedures. The trainer allows individuals and crews to rehearse and physically execute the necessary steps.

During my time at Camp Atterbury in Indiana, I participated in HEAT. I was placed in the front right passenger seat, with a very large piece of navigational equipment next to me leaving very little space to move. During the course of the training, we did a 180-degree roll. I became claustrophobic, riddled with anxiety, and tried to get out of the vehicle but could not. My heart raced and I hyperventilated, pulling desperately on the door lever to escape the vehicle. After about sixty seconds of attempting to egress the vehicle, I was able to get the attention of the lead instructor. He realized I needed immediate help and assisted me with getting out of the vehicle. I was diaphoretic, pale, my hands crippled with carpel spasms and my stomach wrecked with waves of nausea. I began to breathe, slowly attempting to center myself and regain control of my mind and body. The senior enlisted trainer and I walked outside for about ten minutes. He provided words of encouragement, and I started to reclaim control over my breathing and anxiety. I knew I needed to get back into this vehicle as soon as possible to complete the training; this was a requirement for entrance into the combat theater. I climbed back into the HEAT, and with some moderate difficulty I was able to complete the training successfully.

I did not give the incident of the storm any additional thought. However, a few days later, I was driving and felt an overwhelming sense of uneasiness. My heart was racing, palms sweating, and I couldn't breathe. What the hell was this? I immediately called my brother; he sensed the panic in my voice. He asked where I was and told me to come by his office. When I walked in, I was shaking, my palms cold and clammy, and my knees weak. I sat on the floor, put my head on his lap, and cried uncontrollably. I could only imagine what my brother was thinking. He took my hand looked me in the eye, and said, "I've got you, my sister. It's safe here, I love you,

Imperfections

you're not in the combat zone or anywhere else in the world, and this is going to pass. Please breathe and rest easy. It's safe here."

After about twenty minutes, I was able to collect myself and went on about my day. I continued to have these episodes daily for a week, and then weekly for about a month. At some point, I realized I had PTSD. I had PTSD. Another emotional loop of hell. I paused in the moment and realized the possible triggers: fear, lack of gracefulness, lack of love and belonging. I meditated on the anxiety and honestly admitted to myself the trigger was fear. The fear of failing was the driving force, and this would require investigation and forgiveness. I controlled the triggers with a healthy wellness-based lifestyle. I truly believe anyone who has served in combat zone probably has a form of PTSD.

Calming your inner voice is an enduring learning process. Again, pause in the stillness, reflecting on the triggers of anxiety and fear. Embrace imperfections. Say mantras, remain open in the moment, vulnerable and ultimately free the fear of imperfection. Practice quieting the inner voice and allow all energy to flow through you. Being uncomfortable is a process you

The Coefficient of Grace

have to learn to work through, and it requires keeping an open heart and allowing the uncomfortable to pass. Remember, uncomfortable is a variable, and what you choose to do with a variable is your choice. Michael Alan Singer, a writer, philosopher, and yogi, has two works, *The Untethered Soul* and *The Surrender Experiment*. Both have been very helpful to me on my journey. These two works emphasize understanding of self, balance, and calming the chaos. I recommend any of the works by author Michael Singer, Mark Nepo, and the Dalai Lama. I have learned to pray daily, be present, focused, and not distracted, ultimately managing fears and anxiety so I can have a harmonious life and a joyful heart.

Anger

ANGER IS A BASIC HUMAN EMOTION and is directly linked to the fight-or-flight response driven by the old brain. Anger must be monitored by self-awareness and should never erupt into hostility or violence toward others.

After the divorce, my friends and colleagues wanted to know why I was not angry with my ex-husband. I spoke with my therapist, and she encouraged me to meditate and reflect on anger. As I began thinking about anger, I wrote following:

As I reflect on what was, I could be angry, but I am not. I could be consumed with regret, but I am not. I am grateful for the time we had. I hold no malice against anyone, not even my ex-husband. People change and grow in different directions. In hindsight, there were many non-negotiable independent variables that were superimposed and drove us apart, and over time I have come to realize it is OK. Somewhere late in 2015, after the divorce, I was struggling with emotional transitions; the changes were many and overwhelmed my ability to remain clear in thought. In addition, I struggled with not being angry; why am I not angry? Am I supposed to be angry? Is something wrong with me and that is why I am not angry? Is the plan for me to be angry and resentful? Am I expected to despise myself and to accept all of the blame? Meaning I would have to own all emotions. The journey is not as expected.

In 2015, once the divorce proceedings were completely over, I focused my energy on positive things. I returned to school to obtain my master's degree in nursing, specifically to become an adult gerontology acute care nurse practitioner. This was a difficult choice and a huge commitment in time, especially when I was distracted. The divorce was a distraction and my fear of failing was an obstacle. I would need to navigate around obstacles to confront my fear. I had to clear my heart and continue to forgive myself. I needed to end my fight-or-flight responses and employ clear, unemotional thought, self-forgiveness, and gracefulness. I needed to be present in the now. The support of my family, my life sisters, and my newly acquired ability to focus on all things good became my saving grace. Being brave and courageous was hard, but failing was a tougher and unacceptable outcome.

Through my experience with divorce, I learned to practice being graceful of self, and of others, and to live life with intention. Put simply: every day is a gift. Be kind, pay life forward, be generous, expect nothing in return, and do not hold on to anger. Remember to pause before responding, and do not allow anger to perpetuate. If anger becomes problematic, seek assistance in understanding and managing.

Lessons in anger are important. Once anger is understood, then the journey shifts to understanding how not to be angry. Learn techniques to affirm and express your feelings calmly and directly without becoming defensive, hostile, or emotionally charged.

Seek to understand why you are angry and determine why you need to respond to everything. No one is obligated to answer. If it is only to win the war or to be right, then I suggest pausing and seeking an understanding. Be graceful in the tough times. Being right only means you are right, and ultimately that's all you are left with.

Forgiveness

THE DIVORCE WAS A CHALLENGE, as there were no discussions, no conversations—just divorce papers and lawyers. The unexpected change required emotional transition. Forgiveness became the goal, but how? One emotional event at a time, one day at a time; thank goodness for family, a few great friends, and therapy. My therapist encouraged me to write thoughts, feelings, emotions, and daily mantras to find ways to navigate the stormy dark waters of this not-so-unexpected journey. My therapist challenged me to learn who I was—not who everyone else wanted me to be. I reminisced on the recurrent patterns of my life, and the sea was my mantra. I focused on the renewal and regrowth.

I desired to see life from the top of the mountain instead of being in a boat looking up. Somewhere along this trajectory, it became very clear that I was missing joy, balance, and harmony—my reasons for being me.

Forgiveness myself was the first step in finding joy. I had to forgive myself for imperfections in my life that made me feel unworthy.

I began to find my breath in the chaos, and then let it all go. Therapy encouraged me to write the things I liked and did not like about myself and my life. I reviewed the list and determined what was mine to own and what I was able to change; the other things I needed to let go. This list was under constant revision and adjustment. I still make lists on an as-needed basis. It's important to understand external change and internal transitions are a daily process. Practicing mindfulness is necessary, as are understanding loss and letting it go.

In order to forgive yourself, pause and be still. Calm your inner voice. Make time for honest self-reflection with an intent on healthy self-talk. Make a list of the things you like and don't like about your life. Identify the things you can modify and the things you cannot. Make the conscious decision to eliminate the negative things and develop a how-to plan. Think of this as spring cleaning of your heart.

Joy and Happiness

JOY INVOLVES A STATE OF POSITIVITY, where a person experiences feelings of freedom, safety, and the ease of life. According to the *Merriam-Webster* dictionary, "joy is the emotion evoked by well-being, success, good fortune, or by the prospect of possessing what one desires." Regardless of where you are on the spectrum of joy and happiness, each person has their own definition. Eleanor Roosevelt said, "Someone once asked me what I regarded as the three most important requirements for happiness. My answer was: A feeling that you have been honest with yourself and those around you; a feeling that you have done the best you could both in your personal life and in your work; and the ability to love others."

Joy and happiness are a wondrous gift. Regrettably, when feelings of joy and happiness are experienced, we hedge our bets and prepare for tragedy. It's so easy to sabotage these wonderful feelings by defaulting to a preprogrammed mindset of waiting on the next bad event to happen. This occurs partly because we have lost our tolerance for vulnerability, love, kindness, and the ability to live fully in the present. Like the special man once articulated to me so eloquently, "live in the moment with focus and not distraction."

One day, after church service on a Sunday, my chaplain reminded me of what the Psalmist said: "Weeping may endure for a night, but joy comes in the morning." Remember that the journey of grace, forgiveness, and joy begins with healing.

For me, healing required crying, lots and lots of crying. Crying is not a weakness, but it is the cleansing of the heart and soul. Joel Osteen noted, "God will turn your mourning into dancing. Tears of sorrow will turn into tears of joy." Sharing positive experiences leads to increased feelings of joy and happiness.

Joy and Happiness

Drawing attention to the positive things in our lives radically improves our health and well-being. Having an attitude of gratitude improves an individual's ability to connect with others. For example, tell someone you need them, you love them, and they are important to you. This is not a sign of weakness but a sign of strength.

My husband at the time told me told every day for about six years that I could never run the Army Ten Miler; I was not capable of running ten miles, I did not have the stamina, nor did I possess emotional fortitude to complete it. At some point, I began to believe I wasn't capable.

In May of 2014, I decided to challenge myself, in the face of years of emotional turmoil, to run the Ten Miler. I trained, and every day in the gym was mentally and physically tough. I was pushed further than I thought I could go. Jumping, pushing sleds, running stairs, and more. I was developing mental, spiritual, and emotional strength, which led to feelings of happiness and accomplishment.

On October 10, 2014, standing at the starting line, fear and self-doubt filled me. The cannon sounded the start of the race. The Army Ten Miler had begun. The first seven miles of the race went by quickly and effortlessly. At mile seven into mile eight, I realized I was actually running the entire race. My eyes filled with tears, and I looked to my left and my right in awe. All of us were running for different reasons and causes, but *we* were running the Army Ten Miler. I completed the race in under one hour and fifty minutes and have completed the race four additional times since 2014. Don't ever let anyone ever tell you what you cannot do; no one else can define you. You can do whatever you put your mind, body, and spirit to.

Life is about having the strength and the courage to be in the moment without fear, guilt, shame, or weakness. Understanding what joy and happiness is to you allows you to move forward with positive energy and focus. In my moment of self-doubt filled with negativity, my brother told me to be strong and do what was in my heart. We must learn to walk the wire of life with vulnerability and kindness. Understanding the human consequence, overcoming years of verbal naysaying and emotional barriers allows you to lean into joy and be grateful for life's blessings. If not for

Joy and Happiness

my friends and colleagues who trained with me, held my hand, and stood by me, I am not sure I would have had the confidence to complete the race. Life's connections are true blessings.

Connecting with others with positive affirmations is important to a life filled with joy and happiness. You can have comfort or courage, but not both simultaneously. Having the courage to say I love you first is not weakness but a strength. Admittedly, there is a degree of uncertainty in saying I love you first. However, take the risk and connect with love and trust, and share happiness and joy.

The one true currency in this insolvent world is inner harmony of a joyful heart. It is not the number of things you own or things you can buy, but clarity and harmony in which you live. Promise yourself to always characterize yourself in a positive, gentle, and thoughtful way. Be vulnerable to your needs first. It is very easy to take care of others' needs, but learn to pause and quiet the inner voice to understand happiness and joy.

Fabulous You

IN MAY OF 2016, I SPENT FOURTEEN DAYS on the Isle of Nevis, sitting by the pool and absorbing the wonderful rays of the sun. I was away from all negative energy, work-related obligations, and life's distractions. I read many books while breathing in the ocean air and recalibrating my sense of purpose. It was here where I learned that fabulous was a state of mind and the catalyst for bridging change. Fabulous is fundamentally different for each individual. For me, fabulous was the term I used for my voyage of internal and external acceptance.

I will attest that facing internal demons is more difficult than external demons. The inside voice consumed my positive energy. Constant change and the lack of emotional transition stole inner balance and facilitated the downward out-of-control spiraling of emotions. Life became about existing in a world deprived of clear thought or focused purpose. In 2013, when my friend pointed out that the light and love in my heart was gone and the essence of all things "Rena" had been extinguished, I realized I'd forgotten how to be a me—a woman, a sexy, vulnerable, beautiful woman. Now, before all the feminists get riled up, hear me out. While serving this great county, you can't be too pretty or too unpretty. You typically don't wear a lot of makeup; hair has to be worn in a certain way, and it is exhausting figuring out what you can and can't wear in each uniform. Not an excuse—just compliance with the regulation. When the uniform is no longer the daily dress, military members often struggle with making decisions on what to wear, fashion, how to style hair, how to apply makeup, and so much more. I have spoken to over five hundred women currently serving, and the majority admit to being lost in a store when shopping for themselves. Over half have not been to a spa in ten years or more and admit to being lost at the makeup counter. Most women say that after spending years of their lives wearing what the job required, when they look in the mirror, they have no idea who is looking back. A familiar statement to many, including myself.

I had gained and lost weight over the years and had this large skin fold that was preventing acceptance of my external physical self. I sought consultation with a plastic surgeon. The surgeon and I met on three separate occasions, and he told me the only way to be rid of my "large fold" was to have it surgically removed. I scheduled the surgery in January of 2018 and there was no turning back. The surgery lasted four and a half hours; I woke with multiple surgical drains in place, wearing a very tight body garment. The road to recovery was tough for about three weeks. The drains were removed after a week, and I was able to fit into my normal clothes after two weeks, but body garments needed to be worn for a minimum of twelve weeks. This was a transformative life event, and I would recommend plastic surgery only to those women who have achieved inner peace and balance. It is not for the faint of heart. Within four months,

I felt like a new woman; I could wear a bikini and not worry about tucking in my shirt without feeling conscious about my tummy. The results of the surgery were freeing.

The military is dominated by males, and most women feel the need to prove themselves and be accepted as members of the team. I felt the overwhelming need to exceed the standards and exhausted myself in doing so. In 2009, during the Civil Affairs Qualification Course, a major told me that because I was a female, I had only one chance to impress the brigade commander, and if I blew it, I would be marginalized for the remainder of my career. He went on to remind me that I was a nurse corps officer in a combat environment and that there was no time to be kind or caring—that the 80/20 rule applied, meaning an 80 percent solution was good enough.

I was shocked and disheartened by this rhetoric. I paused and respectfully reminded the major that my job as a nurse had nothing to do with being female or a captain. That if he had been injured and hemorrhaging from an amputation of his leg, and I stopped the bleeding by applying direct pressure with the application of a tourniquet, I would prevent his death, but if his heart wasn't beating, he'd be dead. That in my world, 80/20 was an unacceptable solution set. Needless to say, the conversation ended, and there were no additional discussions regarding my competence as a nurse, a captain, or a member of the Civil Affairs Team. This was a moment of external validation.

As a soldier and leader, you have to be assertive and speak with a valid, informed, and authentic voice. However, in the civilian sector, this assertiveness is often interpreted as aggressive or bitchy. Remaining graceful and empathetic across varied situations, acting in multiple roles (military/civilian nurse/leader) is often difficult. To be graceful, yet assertive, necessitates balance and self-awareness, the self-awareness to look through a different lens and realize how others perceive you.

In the military, specifically the Army, the uniform is armor—it protects us and often prevents individual feelings of "fabulousness." There are certain accepted and expected behaviors while in uniform, and at times that makes it difficult to be human. The ability to keep up with constant change and the internal emotional challenges are fundamental. The obstacles of the human consequence have to be negotiated. Unfortunately, sometimes the process of traversing obstacles leaves individuals always armored up and without happiness or joy.

Life's internal or external obstacles can prevent us from being the best versions of ourselves. Fabulous is not about the final product; it is more about the things we learn along the way, the people we meet, the experiences that bring life meaning. We are not defined by the uniforms or our roles in life. The choices we make daily impact the future. Avoid getting caught up in work, daily annoyances, drama, roadblocks, and other life challenges. Do not allow these challenges to make you miserable. Learn to reframe them as opportunities. It is a conscious choice to define your fabulousness and your life's purpose.

Spaces In Between

THROUGHOUT THIS BOOK, breathing has been mentioned in every section. Learning to breathe is a vital part of life but is also representative of a harmonious balance. I took a scuba course in the summer of 2015. The divorce was complete and I was learning to live again freely without reservations and enjoying the freedom to fail without being judged. I soon learned this was part of the healing process.

Water is peaceful and represents quietness and healing. The course started out in the pool. Performing scuba in the pool was easy. I'm comfortable in the water. I grew up in the pool, swimming four to six hours a day, so breathing through the apparatus was second nature. I had control and knew assistance was only an arm's reach away, much like my team in the Afghanistan. The challenge came in the open water.

We arrived at the quarry in late August. The class began preparations for the open-water dive. Filled with significant trepidation, I positive self-talked and was able to calm my fears and anxiety. The class entered the water with buddy systems in place. I could sense my anxiety increasing but remained focused on the tasks and kept breathing. The instructors sensed my hesitation and walked me through every step. Once in the water, the group swam to the first test point. I deflated the buoyancy compensator for my first controlled descent in open water; at first it seemed easy—until the face mask began to lose sunlight and the horizon filled with a view from underwater. Anxiety overcame me as I started hyperventilating and found myself longing for comfort and safety. At that moment, I knew what I had been searching for since my return from Afghanistan—balance and control. In a flash, I replayed four years of my life: surviving combat, a divorce, and struggling with emotional transitions.

In that moment, I realized my life was not ending, but beginning. Suddenly, my instructor reached out and grabbed my buoyancy compensator and we came back to the surface together. I removed my mask and took a few deep breaths to regain control of myself. After a few words of encouragement, we descended together. My first few breaths under the surface were freeing, and then once engulfed by the water, I found my balance between inhaling and exhaling. As the air filled in my lungs, my diaphragm expanded and contracted with every breath. I could feel everything, and it was surreal and freeing. I was experiencing a new version of harmony and joy.

Fear of failing was my life obstacle. Regaining control over the overwhelming changes and building bridges to forge a new future was the end state. One of my Army mentors told me when there is a rock blocking the way forward, you have to come up with a focused, unemotional plan to get past it. Using distraction techniques, I was able to focus on physical and emotional well-being and move forward. Distraction techniques are activities that allow the redirection of current emotions. The goal is to reset attention toward something else and move forward. For me distraction techniques were adventures, adventures which provided a path to focused clear thought.

An example of using a distraction technique was in April of 2017, when I trekked for five days in the Andes, followed by a hike into Machu Picchu. This trek was about understanding the spaces in between, without anxiety and emotional discord. I challenged myself emotionally, physically, and spiritually, which provided a path toward self-trust and fabulousness. My life view was forced to change in little moments, like standing between two of the highest peaks in South America, listening to the sounds of glaciers cracking and splintering, of avalanches flowing, all while watching condors flying overhead. In those moments, I realized how insignificant I was and that imperfections don't really matter in this world.

It is important to begin each day with things in your life that matter most. Remind yourself of your priorities. Search for the humbling moments, the constructive distractions, the ones which require you to recalibrate emotional transitions. Seek opportunities for growth and humility. Surround yourself with confident, focused people and endure in the present while focusing on the joy and harmony in your heart.

COVID-19

I AM CURRENTLY DEPLOYED IN GERMANY for a one-year assignment working for European Command in the Joint Operations Center (JOC) as a team chief. God has a unique way of putting us where we need to be. Who would have thought a nurse would be in the JOC during a global pandemic? Not a typical assignment for a nurse corps officer. But here I am.

I was tasked as the JOC lead for Task Force COVID, which required coordinating all information across European Command, providing guidance to senior leaders, coordinating products, and submitting reporting requirements to the joint staff, all while working in a top-secret compartmentalized environment.

When the stop movement order went into place, I was upset, because the one person in this world I wanted to see I could not. It was external change disrupting internal emotional transition. It was imperative I did not allow this to consume me. Much like in Afghanistan and through my divorce, I found ways to prevent fight-or-flight responses. I performed daily self-checks to evaluate my own selfish wants and desires, and I understood God needed me elsewhere.

I learned COVID and combat were similar. Self-isolation required strong mental clarity with focused presence. It was difficult. Several members of the team tested positive for COVID and were placed in isolation. The team shifted to essential staffing only, meaning we worked three days on and six days off. The amount of alone time was difficult. I was only able to drive to and from work, shop on assigned days, and had to learn to navigate boredom and mental anguish. I performed physical training and yoga daily to ward off anxiety and fear. Remaining focused with purpose was the key, much like my return home from Afghanistan ten years prior. I needed to use the skills I'd acquired: using grace, practicing forgiveness, and searching for joy and happiness in simple things. Sunrises, birds singing, and text messages from family and the special man have kept me sane.

On day twelve of self-isolation, in a vulnerable state, I was talking with the special man. I told him I loved him. I didn't expect those words to come out of my mouth, but they did. I began to cry, panicked, and said I'm sorry. I fumbled far worse than a quarterback in the Superbowl. I was falling on my sword, trying to regain composure. This was a flight response. What the hell was happening to me? Clearly a lack of self-trust and vulnerability. I was afraid. Afraid he would run away and disappear. Good hell, I thought, just breathe, it's OK. I quieted my mind and calmed the anxiety. The special man who I met about a year before on a military tour kindly reaffirmed he was not going anywhere and reassured me he was going to stand and wait for me to get to him. He also said that this event shouldn't prevent me from crushing my sphere at work. Easier said than done, my inside voice bellowed.

I reflected on this event for a few days and realized my ability to be unarmored allowed me to be me—I mean, be really me! Not a nurse, not an Army officer, but me, Rena: a graceful, joyful, and beautiful person. It took courage and strength to be vulnerable.

Regardless of my vulnerable moment, I had a job to do and a mission to support. This required me to be present in all aspects. My focus and diligence were what were needed, not me being distracted by the words said from my heart.

The command-directed alone time provided space to reflect on who I am and what I want in this life. I was learning about myself again. I realized I am a social creature and require human and animal interaction. While out on my social distancing activities, seeing a dog makes me smile. God has reminded me of his greatness every time I see things like birds singing melodies or the trees swaying back and forth, rocking like our mothers when we were children, to sooth our hearts and ease our souls. God places us where we need to be, when we need to be there. For the first time in my life, I did not see myself for my imperfections or failures. My journey brought me here. Elevated me to have the ability to see beyond the boat, to look upward to understand and navigate the ebb and flow of life with minimal fear and anxiety. Colonel Jim Allen speaks often about time. "It is really all about time and what we do with time. Time is perplexing but necessary." I have thought many hours about time and what we do with it.

What is profoundly missing during this COVID pandemic is human interaction. My wells get filled with human touch, which is not authorized. I miss holding my patients' hands, providing support to those in need, making a difference in people's lives. I miss my family, my best friends, and the special man.

My long-time friend Andrea Allen wrote in March of 2020, which she later shared with me in April 2020: "Perhaps this is a time for the world to regroup and rebirth. Knowing that the Mother Earth will take care of us and enlightenment of an entire society waits. We are being asked to be in our homes. Our 'cocoon.' Butterflies are deep and powerful representations of life. Many cultures associate the butterfly with our souls. Like the caterpillar to the butterfly, our individual selves and society as a whole will be forever changed when we emerge."

If we learn anything from this pandemic, it's that human consequence is real. It has no boundaries, no country, and it knows no prejudice. It does not favor one side or the other. It is not political, and we should not make it so. It is a time for the world to come together and fight the good fight. Understand how to manage your fear and anxiety. Do we feel anxiety because we are not in control, fear because we are scared for our loved ones, panic because the life we knew might be forever changed? We must pause and reflect on external change and focus on internal recalibration. Calm your anxiety, listen to your inner voice, open your eyes, and choose to see treasured gifts. The keys to an inner harmony and a joyful heart is to quiet the inner voice, to stand strong in the storm, pause to breathe, and seek understanding of change and emotional transitions.

Conclusion

I'M NOW FIFTY-FOUR and continue to work on being graceful, brave, courageous, and vulnerable. I would say being uncomfortable and vulnerable are the hardest to accomplish. How we manage fear and anxiety helps shape us as individuals. In order to be brave, courageous, and uncomfortable, you have to be vulnerable. Having success or failure is purely a variable that you can manage. Managing variables (for me, fear and anxiety) can lead to a joyous heart and a harmonious life.

What I have learned since my return from Afghanistan is to pause and calm my inner voice. I've had to recognize anxiety and fear and understand where these emotions come from, while also recognizing when life shifts and seeking to balance emotional transitions.

In December of 2019, I cared for a patient who was thirty-three years old. He had been diagnosed with esophageal cancer, had undergone tumor debulking surgery, and was receiving palliative chemotherapy and radiation. I met this young man during a rapid response. Rapid response is called by nursing when a patient has had a dynamic change or rapid decline in their medical condition. Tim had a rapid decline in his respiratory status. He did not have an advanced directive, nor had he discussed his end-of-life wishes with his family. I entered his room, and found he was breathing fifty-five times per minute, oxygen saturations were falling, and he was using accessory muscle to breathe. He was in serious trouble; he would need airway and oxygen support. I began to critically think through the problem. First was to address the obvious: Did he want to be intubated and placed on a ventilator? And if the answer was no, then what? I ordered an arterial blood gas and asked the staff to

Conclusion

call the intensivist. I held his hand and, while looking in his eyes, asked him if he wanted a tube placed in his lungs to help his breathing. With what energy he had, he said no. I then ordered a bi-level positive airway pressure, a noninvasive way to support his increasing oxygen requirements, and morphine to ease his breathing. His heart rate was elevated, blood pressure stable, and he remained alert and cognizant of his surroundings. His mother was at the bedside, standing silently, eyes filled with tears and struggling to understand what was happening. I attempted to calm her with simple factual explanations, all while providing emotional support. The intensivist arrived, and we reviewed the chart and discussed options for care. Tim was breathing more easily and oxygen levels were improving. We completed the Do Not Intubate or Resuscitate form, allowing natural death if his condition deteriorated. This was emotionally difficult for everyone; this was a thirty-three-year-old man, father of two children, ages four and seven. Over the course of the next three days, after rounding on my assigned patients, I would check in with nursing, Tim, and his family. Visiting with patients and family became the highlight of my days. Tim always took my hand and had me sit at his bedside, and his family always welcomed me with hugs. On day three, Tim had begun transitioning, moving toward the end of life. I worked with nursing and the attending physician to manage the sometimes uncomfortableness of this process—the gasping for breath and overall anxiety. He was on a morphine drip, but the current dosages were not managing his symptoms. I walked to the nursing station to speak with nursing and make adjustments to the medications, and the chaplain was there. The chaplain and I discussed Tim's status, prognosticating he had minutes to hours before he passed. The chaplain immediately went to the room; I gave him a few minutes, and then I re-entered the room. It was 16:45; the family was there. Tim reached for my hand, and I sat at his bedside, where he peacefully passed at 16:47.

Afghanistan and twenty-six years of nursing could not prepare me for repeated losses, unexpected change, and emotional transitions. Standing at Tim's bedside, I realized the last ten years have taught me to understand emotional transitions and to practice grace and

Conclusion

forgiveness of self. My journey has provided me an avenue to a harmonious life and a joyful heart.

Throughout life, I believe, we all try to make a difference, both individually and collectively. The teams in Afghanistan, medical teams, and people in everyday life. Even if it is only for a moment in time, we make a difference! I was reminded of how much we make a difference at Tim's beside. Being there with him and his family as he passed was a simple and final act of kindness to him and to me.

I am grateful for my ability to serve this great country as an Army nurse corps officer and as a nurse serving the sick, ill, and injured.

I hope this book helps you on your journey to find your inner harmony and joyful heart. I remain committed to hard work and dedication to self and caring for others. I work daily to manage fears of failure as old habits and life patterns die a long slow death.

See and be seen. Be vulnerable where you stand. Be courageous. Be fearless. Be amazing and fabulous. You got this! You are special, you are worthy, and every day is worth living.

Bibliography

Lama, Dalai. *The Art of Happiness: A Handbook for Living.* New York: Penguin Group, 1998.

Nepo, Mark. *The Exquisite Risk: Daring to Live an Authentic Life.* New York: Three Rivers Press, 2005.

Singer, Michael A. *The Untethered Soul: A Journey Beyond Yourself.* Oakland: New Harbinger Publications, 2007.

Singer, Michael A. *The Surrender Experiment: My Journey into Life's Perfection.* New York: Penguin Random House, 2015.

"Theory of Human Caring." Watson Caring Science Institute. Updated 2020.

www.watsoncaringscience.org.

Acknowledgements

Thank you to my life sentinels: my brother John Patierno, sister-in-law Andrea Patierno, nieces, Katelyn, Ashley, Avery, and nephew, Joey, whose love and support have never wavered. My best girlfriends, Janene Ciotti, Emily Baez, Tatiana Belijac and Dawn Williams: Thank you for always believing and never doubting. Your unconditional love has been the light in the darkness. Thank you for always loving me, even when I was not so lovable. To my military family: Sebastein Kravitz, Major General Dave Morris (retired), Colonel Bob Whaley (retired), Colonel Scott Johnson, Colonel Gail Fisher, Colonel Charlie Johnson (retired), Colonel Philip Good (retired), Colonel James Allen, Colonel Russ Rybka, Colonel Christopher "Roll Tide" Murphy, Lieutenant General Michael Howard, Brigadier General Christian Wortman, Mr. L. Fetterman, the soldiers of the Potomac Recruiting Company 2013–2019, Pat Powers, Jonathon Wilder, nursing colleagues, and my treasured family. I am truly blessed. Your love and friendship is one of the greatest gifts.

My life has not been the typical American dream, but that is the beauty of America. Nothing is typical and everything is possible. My parents always taught me to try something new, give your best, and never quit. If you have given your best, your honest best, then you can walk away with a clean heart. My parents allowed my brother and me to find our own way. We were allowed to experience all types of life, religions, and cultures. We were encouraged to carve out our own relationships with God and our own life paths. We were encouraged to see people as people, not see the differences, but see the greatness. The humanity, the grace, and the gifts. We were taught to be humble and kind from a very young age. Selfless service, humility, and grace were the foundation for our family and our lives. For this I am truly grateful.

About the Author

Rena Patierno is a New York native with more than twenty-five years of nursing experience and nineteen years of service in the U.S. Army Reserve as a nurse corps and civil affairs officer. She is an Afghanistan combat veteran and the recipient of the French National Defense Medal. Rena holds a master's degree in nursing and is a board-certified adult gerontology acute care nurse practitioner. Currently, Rena is fighting the COVID Crisis for European Command as a Joint Operation.

www.ingramcontent.com/pod-product-compliance
Lightning Source LLC
Chambersburg PA
CBHW072206100526
44589CB00015B/2391